Just the Facts
# Child Labour
Kaye Stearman

Heinemann
LIBRARY

**www.heinemann.co.uk/library**
Visit our website to find out more information about **Heinemann Library** books.

To order:
 Phone 44 (0) 1865 888066
 Send a fax to 44 (0) 1865 314091
 Visit the Heinemann Bookshop at www.heinemann.co.uk/library to browse our catalogue and order online.

**Produced by Monkey Puzzle Media Ltd**
Gissing's Farm, Fressingfield, Suffolk IP21 5SH, UK

First published in Great Britain by Heinemann Library, Halley Court, Jordan Hill, Oxford OX2 8EJ, part of Harcourt Education.
Heinemann is a registered trademark of Harcourt Education Ltd.

Editorial: Sarah Eason and Georga Godwin
Design: Mayer Media
Picture Research: Lynda Lines
Production: Edward Moore

Originated by Dot Gradations Ltd
Printed and bound in Hong Kong, China by
 South China Printing Company

ISBN 0 431 16161 5
08 07 06 05 04
10 9 8 7 6 5 4 3 2 1

This text has been checked by UNICEF for factual accuracy, but this is not a UNICEF publication and it does not necessarily reflect the views or policy of UNICEF.

**British Library Cataloguing in Publication Data**
Stearman, Kaye
Child Labour
331.3'1
A full catalogue record for this book is available from the British Library.

**Acknowledgements**
The publishers would like to thank the following for permission to reproduce photographs:
AKG London pp. **9** (Musée Condé), **10** (Lewis W. Hine); Associated Press p. **26** (Erick Christian Ahounou); Corbis pp. **44 right** (Tim Pannell); Mark Henley pp. **4–5**, **6**, **18**, **24**, **31**, **42**; Hulton Archive pp. **11**, **15** (Lewis W. Hine); Mary Evans Picture Library p. **12**; Panos Pictures pp. **14** (Fernando Moleres), **19** (Jean-Leo Dugast), **20–21** (Morris Carpenter), **43** (Peter Barker); Popperfoto pp. **13**, **25** (AFP), **30** (Kamal Kishore/Reuters); Press Association pp. **37** (EPA), **38–39** (EPA); Rex Features pp. **7** (Paul Quayle), **16–17** (Today), **28–29** (David Browne); Still Pictures p. **23** (Mark Edwards), **27** (Gerard and Margi Moss), **34–35** (John Isaac), **40** (Ron Giling), **41** (Joerg Boethling), **44 left** (M. Cottingham/Christian Aid), **47** (Hartmut Schwarzbach), **48** (Ron Giling); Topham Picturepoint p. **32–33** (ImageWorks).

Cover photograph reproduced with permission of Mark Henley.

Every effort has been made to contact copyright holders of any material reproduced in this book. Any omissions will be rectified in subsequent printings if notice is given to the publishers.

Any words appearing in the text in bold, **like this**, are explained in the Glossary.

# Contents

# Childhood and adulthood

Children work all over the world. This is not a new situation. In the past, most children had to work to ensure their family's survival and this is still the main reason why children work today. In our own society, many older children work, at home or in part-time casual jobs after school, at weekends or during school holidays. Many people feel this is a good thing, because it teaches children about the value of money, helps them learn useful skills and encourages them to take responsibility. But work is only a small part of life for these children. The world of full-time work belongs to adulthood.

When does childhood end and adulthood start? In most countries there are different ages for leaving school, driving a car, marrying, drinking alcohol, voting and so on. For example, in some US states, a young person can drive at sixteen and vote at eighteen but must wait until twenty-one to drink alcohol legally. And although many countries allow pupils to leave school at fifteen or sixteen, increasing numbers stay on until they are eighteen or nineteen then go on to further studies.

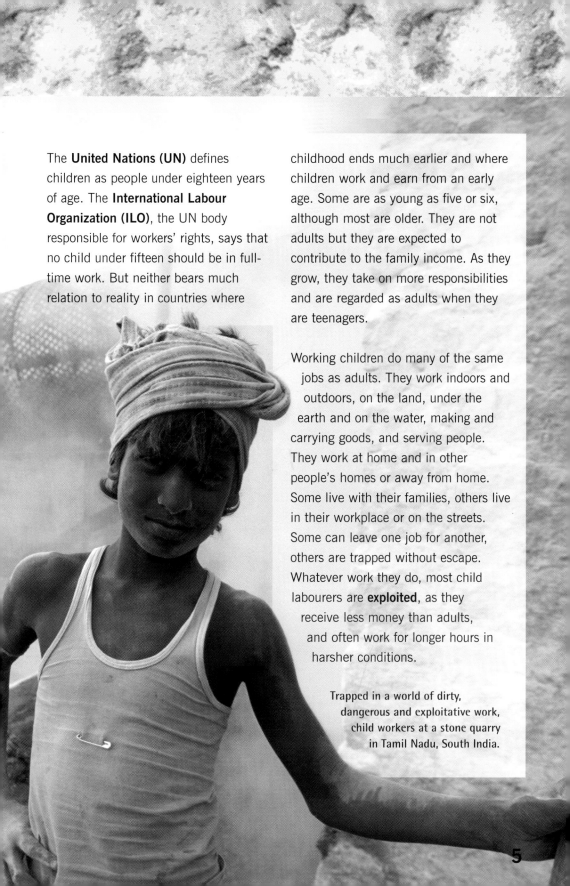

The **United Nations (UN)** defines children as people under eighteen years of age. The **International Labour Organization (ILO)**, the UN body responsible for workers' rights, says that no child under fifteen should be in full-time work. But neither bears much relation to reality in countries where childhood ends much earlier and where children work and earn from an early age. Some are as young as five or six, although most are older. They are not adults but they are expected to contribute to the family income. As they grow, they take on more responsibilities and are regarded as adults when they are teenagers.

Working children do many of the same jobs as adults. They work indoors and outdoors, on the land, under the earth and on the water, making and carrying goods, and serving people. They work at home and in other people's homes or away from home. Some live with their families, others live in their workplace or on the streets. Some can leave one job for another, others are trapped without escape. Whatever work they do, most child labourers are **exploited**, as they receive less money than adults, and often work for longer hours in harsher conditions.

Trapped in a world of dirty, dangerous and exploitative work, child workers at a stone quarry in Tamil Nadu, South India.

5

# The global picture

No one really knows how many children work on a regular basis. Some governments deny that child labour is a problem or say that numbers are either exaggerated or declining. Others admit that there is a problem but do not know how many children are involved. Working children are often hidden from public view, in homes, factories and farms.

However, the **ILO** collects statistics and makes regular estimates of the numbers of working children. The results are startling. Worldwide almost 250 million children aged between 5 and 17 (that's one child in six) are workers, with 179 million (one child in eight) doing jobs that are classed as difficult, dangerous and unsuitable. This figure does not include normal work around the home, like washing up or cleaning the car, or part-time paid work, like a newspaper round or babysitting. It means working for long hours without a break for wages that are minimal, irregular or even non-existent.

So, where are these children? Why don't we see them in the everyday world around us? We may know a few of them, although they probably do not attend school regularly and drop out early. But only about one per cent of working children come from the wealthy countries of North America, Western Europe, Japan and Australasia, with another one per cent from the former Soviet Union. The remaining 98 per cent live in Asia, Africa, Latin America and the Middle East.

A face in the crowd – a teenager pulls a cart in the rush-hour traffic of Jakarta, Indonesia.

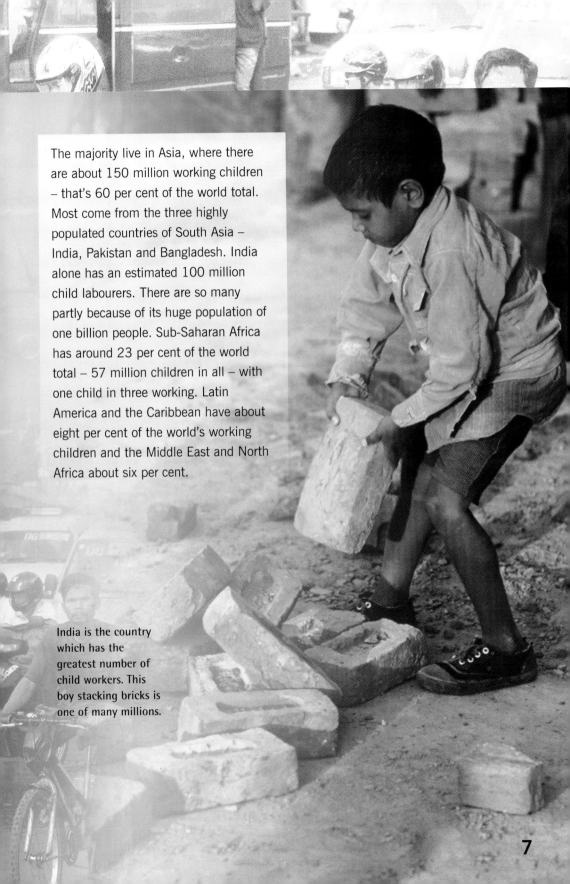

The majority live in Asia, where there are about 150 million working children – that's 60 per cent of the world total. Most come from the three highly populated countries of South Asia – India, Pakistan and Bangladesh. India alone has an estimated 100 million child labourers. There are so many partly because of its huge population of one billion people. Sub-Saharan Africa has around 23 per cent of the world total – 57 million children in all – with one child in three working. Latin America and the Caribbean have about eight per cent of the world's working children and the Middle East and North Africa about six per cent.

India is the country which has the greatest number of child workers. This boy stacking bricks is one of many millions.

# Working for survival

Until fairly recently, most people had to work simply to survive. In this, children were no different from adults. People lived short, active lives and almost everybody laboured – but the labour was tailored to an individual's age and skills. Hunting large animals, directing a heavy plough or grinding grains were hard and heavy jobs reserved for adults. Children did lighter work such as tending animals, collecting water and minding their younger brothers and sisters. Even so, they found time to relax and play. As they grew older they took on more difficult work and by their teenage years were as actively involved in work as adults. In most traditional societies, children followed their parents' occupations, learning from watching and doing rather than formal schooling.

Even so, we know in some societies that children were made to work too long and far too hard. When archaeologists dug at a site in central Turkey called Catal Hoyuk, they found the remains of hundreds of children. Catal Hoyuk was a working community 7500 years ago and the children's bodies suggest that the children had died of exhaustion from long, hard work in the surrounding fields. They may have been slaves or children separated from their families.

**"Country children in general did not go to school; there were few schools and no reason why they should go to them ... The boys would dig the turnips with their father and the girls would reap the corn with their mother. As they all laboured together, the older people would talk to the youngsters."**

*Montaillou – a French village 1294–1324*, Emmanuelle Le Roy Ladurie, 1978

In **medieval** Europe children and adults lived and worked together. From early childhood children wore miniature versions of adult dress. Few went to school or learnt to read and write. Most worked from early childhood in the fields or the great houses of the nobility, often for food and lodging rather than money. Childhood was a perilous time. Without modern medicine or knowledge of basic hygiene, many children died at birth or in early childhood. Those who survived had to be tough enough to work and take on adult responsibilities at an early age.

In medieval Europe peasant children laboured in the fields with the adults and learned valuable skills from them.

# The Industrial Revolutio

The **Industrial Revolution** began in late 18th-century Britain and was the start of a worldwide change in the way people lived and worked. In the 19th century, it spread to Europe, North America and parts of Asia.

By introducing machinery powered by the new methods of water and steam, and later, coal and electricity, factory owners were able to increase production dramatically. Skilled jobs were destroyed and new, less skilled ones were created. For example, hand-woven cloth was replaced by machine-made cloth. Many of the new jobs were

**❝The manufacturers begin to employ children rarely of five years, often of six, very often of seven, usually eight to nine years, [and] the working day often lasted fourteen to sixteen hours exclusive of meals and intervals.❞**

Frederick Engels, *The Condition of the Working Class in England*, 1845

Young children, such as this girl, worked in American factories until the early 20th century.

filled by children, working for long hours in terrible, often life-threatening, conditions.

# The factory system

Even before the rise of large factories, children had worked as **handloom** weavers. But they worked with their families, in their own homes. When demand was high, hours were long but they did not have to work the same long hours every day. The introduction of large factories employing hundreds of people meant that work was **standardized** and strictly supervised. Workers spent hours doing the same monotonous job. Tiny children were employed to operate and maintain the busy machines because they were smaller and more nimble, and also because they were much cheaper than adults.

In the worst cases, orphaned and abandoned children were 'rented out' to factory owners as **'apprentices'**. They lived on the factory premises, were given basic food and clothing and spent all their waking hours at work. The system was so bad that in 1802 the British government passed a law limiting child apprentices in cotton and woollen mills to twelve hours' work a day and banned night work. It was only in 1847 that Parliament limited working hours for children and adults to ten hours a day. Meanwhile thousands of children remained working in textile mills, coal mines and other degrading employment. Many were killed or badly injured. Tiny children were even used as **chimney sweeps**, forced to climb inside tall chimneys thick with soot. It must have been a terrifying experience, alone amid the dirt and darkness.

Children transporting coal in an English coal mine around 1840. In 1842, Parliament passed laws prohibiting young children from working in hazardous conditions underground. By 1923 the ban was extended to children under fourteen.

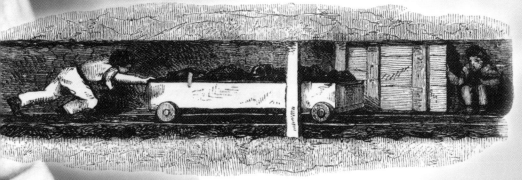

# Reforming the factory system

Not everyone thought that child labour was bad. In the UK, factory owners profited from using child labourers and vigorously defended their role. Most people thought that it was normal for poor children to work to add to the family income. After all, it was not as if there was much else available for children. Only better-off people educated their children, either at home or at school. The only schools for the poorest children were part-time day schools or Sunday schools, and these were often badly run.

However, from the early 19th century people began to speak out against the **exploitation** of factory children. Some men who had lost their jobs to children joined the new **trade unions** to improve wages and working conditions.

**Reformers**, **radical** politicians, **evangelical** ministers, journalists and writers – even a few progressive factory owners – **campaigned** against child labour. Robert Owen, a textile factory owner in Scotland, established a 'model factory' at New Lanark in Scotland which had a nursery and schoolroom for younger children, and light and airy workrooms for older children and adults. Owen's workers were paid fair wages and lived in snug houses.

A scene from the Olympian cotton mills, South Carolina, USA, in 1900, with children working the spinning machines.

Other European countries followed Britain's industrial path and by the end of the 19th century, the USA was rapidly **industrializing**. Millions of poor people from Europe migrated to US cities where they found work in the cotton mills and metal foundries, in giant garment factories and tiny shops, in the stockyards and on the railways. Children often worked long hours in appalling conditions for low wages. Japan also industrialized, with factories employing thousands of teenage girls.

Gradually, however, advances in technology resulted in better and faster machinery, operated by skilled adult workers. This meant there were fewer jobs for young children on the factory floor. More children attended school. Trade unions were gaining recognition and campaigned against child labour. With higher wages and more regular incomes, families in industrialized countries felt less need to send children out to work.

A twelve-year-old 'half-timer' in a textile mill in north-west England in 1920. 'Half-timers' worked only half the day and attended school for the remaining hours.

# From past to present

From the late 19th century onwards, there were two factors above all which kept children from the workforce – legal restrictions and compulsory education. In many **industrializing** countries, including Britain and the USA, there had been fierce opposition to the first laws limiting the hours and type of work that children could do and few inspectors to **enforce** them. However, with time it became widely accepted that young children needed to be protected from **exploitation**, and that governments could do this through stronger laws and better enforcement. Factories had to be inspected regularly and bad employers were taken to court and fined for breaking the laws. In practice, some children slipped through the net but, gradually, in industrialized

In many poor countries, children continue to work in difficult and dangerous jobs. This small girl from Guatemala is collecting plastic for resale.

**❝Child labour remains a problem on a massive scale... The international community still faces a major uphill struggle against this stubbornly pervasive form of work that takes a tragic toll on millions of children around the world.❞**

Juan Somavia, Director-General of the ILO (May 2002)

countries the employment of younger children become less common.

So what happened to the children? The answer is simple. Many more were going to school. A changing industrial society meant people needed new skills and these could only come through formal education. Literacy and numeracy were essential for work and everyday tasks. Governments passed laws making primary, and later secondary, education compulsory and used taxes to fund state education systems. At the beginning of the 20th century children in most Western countries stayed in education until the age of twelve or fourteen – low by today's standards but hugely different from even 50 years earlier.

But child labour hasn't disappeared. Today there are more working children than ever in history. Some of these children work in factories in conditions similar to those of the **Industrial Revolution** but many more are living and working on the land, in small businesses and private homes, and on the streets. Nearly all live in countries where levels of poverty are high, **trade unions** are weak or banned, laws on child labour are non-existent or not enforced and education systems are inadequate or non-existent.

In the USA, as in many other countries, trade unions played an important part in the movement against child labour. This poster from the 1940s was displayed by the Massachusetts United Labor Committee.

Lesson for today

the Labor Unions of America have led the fight to build our free Public School System

the greatest contribution of the labor movement is to the American Public.....

THE MASSACHUSETTS UNITED LABOR COMMITTEE
MASSACHUSETTS AFL, CIO, ADA,
INDEPENDENT UNIONS

PHOTO BY LEWIS W. HINE 1908, COURTESY OF THE RUSSELL SAGE FOUNDATION AND THE PHOTO LEAGUE.

1908    TODAY

# Children in agriculture

Most working children are found in rural areas – planting, weeding and harvesting crops, tending animals, catching and cleaning fish, carrying water. Most of these children work alongside their families, on small farms or large commercial **plantations**. Many children are not full-time workers and some combine light tasks or seasonal work with attending school. Although these children are working, they are not doing tasks that will damage their bodies or their minds.

Yet much agricultural work is dangerous for children. Children may work long hours, spray **pesticides** without wearing protective clothing and use heavy equipment and dangerous tools. Some are injured or suffer long-term health problems. Some children work far from home and family. The wages paid to children are much lower than those for adult workers.

Some of the goods produced by child labour – coffee, cocoa, tea, sugar, fruit and vegetables, fish and seafood – end up on the dinner tables of the rich world. Huge competition forces farmers to produce crops ever more quickly and cheaply. What has made things much worse is that the prices paid for these crops have fallen sharply, so the growers try to get cheaper and cheaper labour. That's why so many children pick beans in the coffee plantations of Central America or labour in the sugar fields of Brazil. That's also why teenage boys travel to the cocoa farms of West Africa or dive for shrimp off the coasts of India and Indonesia.

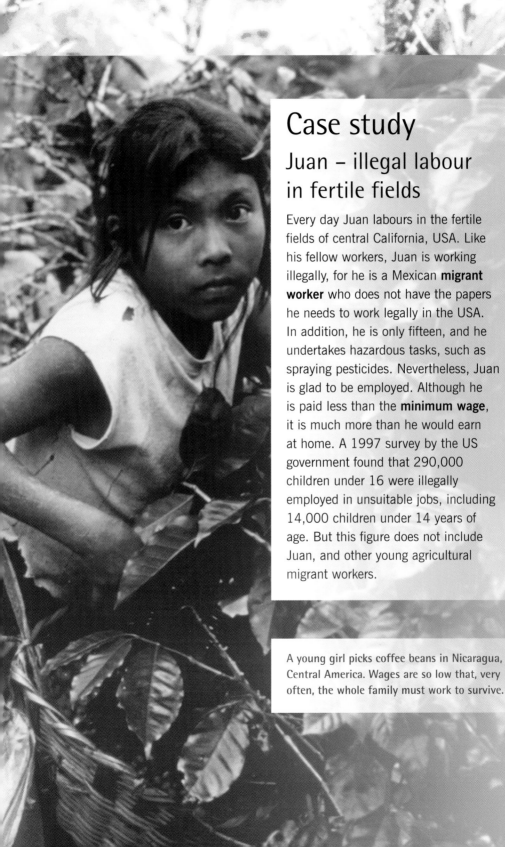

# Case study

## Juan – illegal labour in fertile fields

Every day Juan labours in the fertile fields of central California, USA. Like his fellow workers, Juan is working illegally, for he is a Mexican **migrant worker** who does not have the papers he needs to work legally in the USA. In addition, he is only fifteen, and he undertakes hazardous tasks, such as spraying pesticides. Nevertheless, Juan is glad to be employed. Although he is paid less than the **minimum wage**, it is much more than he would earn at home. A 1997 survey by the US government found that 290,000 children under 16 were illegally employed in unsuitable jobs, including 14,000 children under 14 years of age. But this figure does not include Juan, and other young agricultural migrant workers.

A young girl picks coffee beans in Nicaragua, Central America. Wages are so low that, very often, the whole family must work to survive.

# Children in manufacturing

When we think of child workers, we are most likely to think of children labouring for long hours in factories, like those in the early years of the **Industrial Revolution**. Today, millions of children continue to work in **manufacturing**. Most are in Asia but some are found in Europe and the Americas. For example, the **ILO** reports that young teenagers work in the shoe industry in Portugal.

## Workshops and factories

Most children who work in manufacturing are found in small workshops, working by hand or using simple machinery. They mainly make goods for sale locally, such as bricks, matches, cigarettes, fireworks, glass ornaments and locks. Smaller numbers work in large factories, producing goods (like clothes or shoes) for export abroad. Most do repetitive, unskilled work in poor conditions. Accidents are common and safety regulations are routinely ignored.

## Bonded labourers

In South Asia some children become **bonded labourers**. Bonded labourers are people who have borrowed money from an employer and in return agree to work for them until the loan is repaid. Children often work to repay their parents' debts. Child bonded labourers have been discovered in small carpet workshops in north India and Pakistan. Some work up to twenty hours a day without a break, in tiny, dark rooms. They are deprived of food, are in poor health and often suffer from eye problems.

An open quarry in India where stones are cut and crushed. The children are at risk because the machinery is unsafe and the air is full of dust.

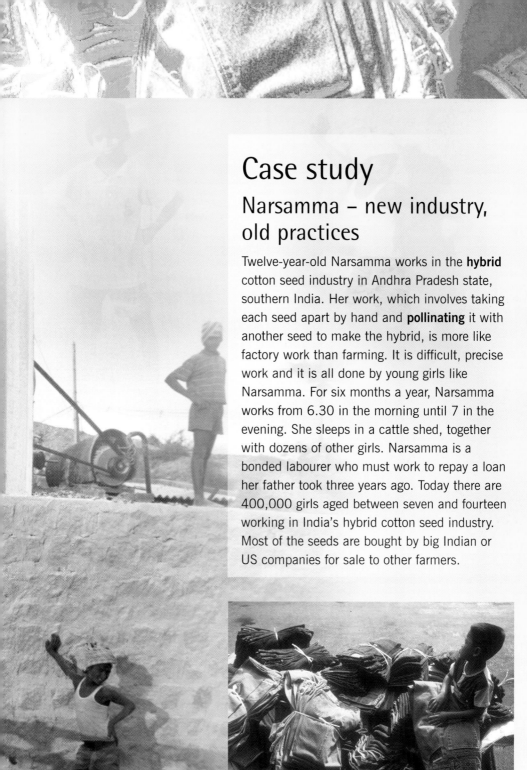

# Case study

## Narsamma – new industry, old practices

Twelve-year-old Narsamma works in the **hybrid** cotton seed industry in Andhra Pradesh state, southern India. Her work, which involves taking each seed apart by hand and **pollinating** it with another seed to make the hybrid, is more like factory work than farming. It is difficult, precise work and it is all done by young girls like Narsamma. For six months a year, Narsamma works from 6.30 in the morning until 7 in the evening. She sleeps in a cattle shed, together with dozens of other girls. Narsamma is a bonded labourer who must work to repay a loan her father took three years ago. Today there are 400,000 girls aged between seven and fourteen working in India's hybrid cotton seed industry. Most of the seeds are bought by big Indian or US companies for sale to other farmers.

A boy sorts and packs jeans in a factory in Thailand.

# Children in domestic service

'Child domestic workers are the world's most forgotten children. They may well be the most vulnerable and **exploited** children of all, as well as the most difficult to protect.' These are the words of the **United Nations** Children's Fund (UNICEF) in their 1997 annual report on child labour.

One of the largest groups of working children work in **domestic service** – they are servants in other people's homes. Around 90 per cent are girls. There is no accurate estimate of their numbers and they are largely overlooked. Many are very young – sometimes only five or six years old – and many live far from their families, never seeing them for months or years. Few attend school.

Poor children work as servants for better-off families. Although they are children themselves, they look after children, wash, cook, clean and serve for incredibly long hours, for small wages or no wages at all. They receive basic food and lodging – often eating leftovers and sleeping on the floor. Some are beaten and abused, physically or sexually. And, whether they are treated well or badly, all lose their childhoods to work.

Where are these child servants? There are millions in South Asia – India, Bangladesh, Pakistan and Nepal. There are millions more in Africa, Latin America and South-east Asia. A few are found in Europe and North America, often teenagers serving wealthy foreign families. But these children are often hidden from sight, so it is difficult to know who they are, where they live or what their lives are like.

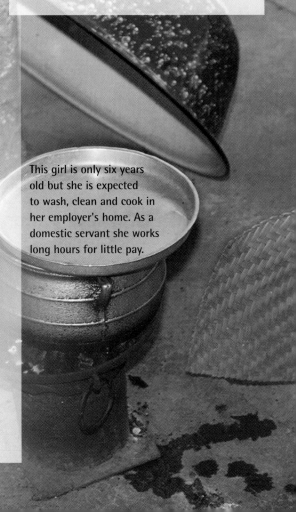

This girl is only six years old but she is expected to wash, clean and cook in her employer's home. As a domestic servant she works long hours for little pay.

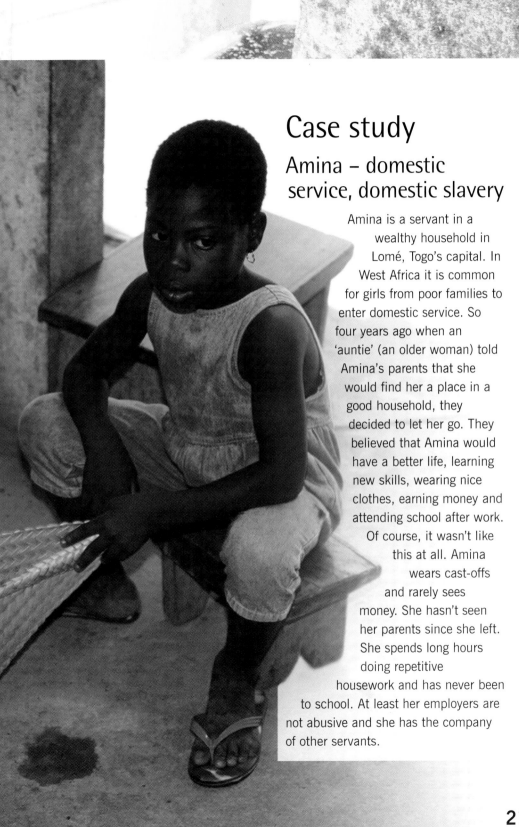

# Case study

## Amina – domestic service, domestic slavery

Amina is a servant in a wealthy household in Lomé, Togo's capital. In West Africa it is common for girls from poor families to enter domestic service. So four years ago when an 'auntie' (an older woman) told Amina's parents that she would find her a place in a good household, they decided to let her go. They believed that Amina would have a better life, learning new skills, wearing nice clothes, earning money and attending school after work. Of course, it wasn't like this at all. Amina wears cast-offs and rarely sees money. She hasn't seen her parents since she left. She spends long hours doing repetitive housework and has never been to school. At least her employers are not abusive and she has the company of other servants.

# Children in shops and catering

In many countries it is easy to spot children selling goods in markets, small shops and on roadsides, or serving customers in tea shops, cafes, restaurants and hotels. Some are working part-time, before or after school or during school holidays. This situation is fairly common in Western countries, where older children and teenagers help out in family stores and other businesses on a part-time basis. These jobs give children skills and responsibilities as well as money.

However, many children throughout the world are forced to work long hours in very tough conditions. They start early and finish late, and work for hours without a break. In India, for example, it is common to see small boys of seven or eight serving customers, clearing tables and washing up late at night. They often live on the premises, far from their families, sleeping on or under tables, and eating left-over food. Like **domestic servants** they may be treated harshly by their masters. However, if conditions are bad, and they have the freedom to move on, they may leave and seek another job, especially as they get older.

## Case study
### Ram – long hours, demanding customers

Eleven-year-old Ram works in a big hotel in a tourist town in southern India. His job is to fetch and carry for customers, to bring them food and drink as and when they order it. The hours are long and the customers are often demanding and bad-tempered. Nevertheless, Ram likes his work and thinks he is lucky. His wage is low but he gets tips from customers. He has a place to sleep, enough to eat and time to chat and play with the other boys working in the hotel. He has learnt a lot about people and the wider world and can even speak some Hindi and English. When he was younger Ram worked in a busy city restaurant, where life was much harder. One day he hopes he will have his own restaurant.

Even children in family-owned shops, like this girl from the Philippines, may find themselves working for hours without a break.

# Children on the streets

Millions of children in **developing countries** work on the city streets. Most have families and many live at home or return home regularly. Others spend all their time on the streets, often banded together in gangs, for friendship and protection. Working on the streets can be dangerous, especially for children without families.

Street children do many types of work, especially providing services to better-off people – carrying bags, running errands, minding parked cars, shining shoes, collecting and sorting rubbish for resale or recycling. Some beg or steal from passers-by. Most have no special skills or equipment, so they learn to become quick and streetwise. They earn very little and they normally spend what they earn each day.

It is nearly always illegal for children to work on the streets but street children say that they have no choice and that it is the only way to survive. Many street children have experienced problems at home – poverty, violence, abuse. Some children become separated from their families during wars, riots or **evictions** and never find their way back home.

Worldwide, boys are more likely to work on the streets than girls, who tend to stay with their families or find work as servants or in factories. But for boys and girls street life is very dangerous. It is common to be cheated, robbed and beaten, run down by cars or arrested by the police. Some children become addicted to glue, alcohol or other drugs

A street child sits on the pavement outside an expensive shoe shop in Mexico City.

or offer sexual services for payment. Street children in South America have even been killed by police to 'clear the streets'. In one 1993 incident in Rio de Janeiro, Brazil, police 'death squads' killed eight street children. Eight years later, two of the children who had survived the massacre in Rio de Janeiro also met violent deaths at the hands of the police.

A three-year-old girl sells cigarettes on the streets of Jakarta, Indonesia. Her role is as much to attract customers as to make sales.

# Case study
## Evans – small children on dangerous streets

In Kenya's capital city, Nairobi, ten-year-old Evans is homeless. He lives and sleeps on the streets of Kibera, Africa's largest slum, with three other boys. Evans has lived like this ever since his home was destroyed in gang fighting. He ran away in the confusion and when he returned found that his family had left Kibera. Now his three friends are his family. They share the money they earn through casual work or begging. Life on the streets is tough and dangerous and they often go hungry. Most of all they fear the police and the criminal gangs who control the slums.

# Trafficking in children

Some types of child labour are so extreme that they can be described as slavery. Child **bonded labourers** are one example. Another is child **trafficking** – where children are removed from their community by violence or deceit and trapped in situations from which they cannot escape.

Growing numbers of children are bought and sold like slaves and taken far away, often to another country. These illegal activities are organized by ruthless criminal gangs, interested only in profit. Trafficking flourishes in areas of extreme poverty and in countries affected by war and conflict. No one knows how many children are involved.

In April 2001 **UN** officials discovered a ship off the West African coast crammed with young children. They were being transported from Togo and Benin to oil-rich Gabon, in central Africa, to become **domestic servants**. This was not the first time this had happened. There had been previous warnings about the trade in young girls and the terrible conditions they endured on the journey and after their arrival.

There have been similar cases elsewhere. For example, thousands of girls have been trafficked from Nigeria and Albania to Italy, to work on the streets. Young girls are smuggled across borders in South-east Asia and sold to brothels. Thousands of children in northern Uganda have been kidnapped by a rebel army. During their captivity, which may last for years, the girls are taken as servants and 'wives' by soldiers, while the boys are forced to become soldiers themselves. It is a bewildering and dangerous life for a trapped and trafficked child.

This young girl faces a bleak future. No one knows how many children have been taken from their families and used as slave labour, unable to escape.

# Case study
## Ali – frightened children far from home

Ali is one of hundreds of young 'camel jockeys' in the Gulf States. Camel racing is a popular activity and small children are considered to make the best riders. Ali was only five when he was taken from his village in Bangladesh and smuggled into the Gulf States. Now he cannot remember his village, his family or even his own native language. It is a terrifying experience being strapped to the racing camel amid the screaming crowds. Some boys are injured or even killed during the races. Although it is now against the law to employ child jockeys the practice still continues and so does the child trafficking.

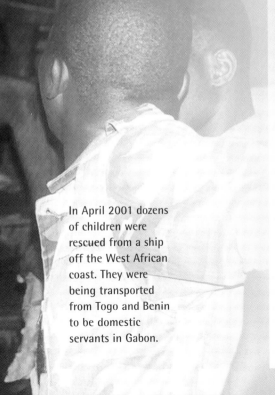

In April 2001 dozens of children were rescued from a ship off the West African coast. They were being transported from Togo and Benin to be domestic servants in Gabon.

# The employers' view

Child labour takes many forms. At best, working children are seen as family assets, their work is valued and they gain skills. At worst, they live like slaves, their work is unpaid and they receive only basic food and lodging. Escape is difficult or impossible and they do not know their rights as either children or workers.

Most working children are not slaves, but they are cheap, easy to control, and easy to hire and fire. So it is not hard to see why some employers want to use child labour. This is especially true in industries where technology is simple and competition is fierce. Making hand-woven carpets is one example.

Employers sometimes argue that children's tiny fingers are especially adept at weaving complex, tight patterns. In fact, the most intricate and expensive carpets are made by skilled adult workers. Children tend to work on lower-quality products.

Employers also favour child labour because children are less able to **strike** or to disrupt production. They are unlikely to know their rights as children or as workers. They find it hard to join **trade unions**, which aim to raise adult wages and are opposed to children working for lower wages. Few working children or employers are known to government inspectors.

28

Some employers justify child labour by pointing out that poor children have few alternatives. In other words, they are doing children a favour by employing them and keeping them away from the dangerous streets. Today this argument has little justification as far as the youngest children are concerned. All countries agree that young children should be in school rather than in work. But what about older children, who have left school, who want and need to work? Many employers would argue that without legal employment they would be pushed into unsafe jobs or on to the streets.

To some extent this is true. Not all employers are bad. In some cases they have been persuaded to move away from child labour and to give existing child workers time off for schooling. But most changes have resulted from outside pressure. As in the early years of the **Industrial Revolution** in Europe and the USA, employers rarely change of their own free will.

Young girls at work in a small match factory in India. Employers prefer children for this work because they are cheap to hire and rarely protest against bad conditions.

29

# The parents' view

Why do some parents send children out to work? Some parents are cruel, abusive or addicted to drugs or alcohol. Others see little value in education and want children to start earning money. In many countries, parents have worked from a young age themselves and expect their children to follow the same path. However, the single most important factor is poverty – children work because their earnings are needed to contribute to family income.

For those living in the West (Europe and the USA) it is hard to appreciate the daily difficulties facing poor families in many parts of Asia, Africa or Latin America. Wages are low and regular jobs are difficult to come by. There are few **benefits** paid by the government, such as child support, unemployment benefit, pensions or insurance schemes to tide people over difficult times. Health and education are rarely free or low-cost so even the poorest people find themselves having to pay the fees charged by hospitals and schools. Poor people find it hard to pay the high prices charged for basic services, like electricity, water or rubbish collection. The result is that even a child's small wages can make a difference to the family income.

A father and his seven-year-old son work together in a stone quarry near New Delhi, the capital of India.

In the most extreme cases, parents may send a child away from home to save the expense of feeding and clothing them. This is the case with many child servants. Often the parents believe that this is for the good of the child, they will learn new skills, become self-supporting and one day return to support other family members. In reality, most children gain only misery and abuse from such experiences, and some lose contact with their families for ever.

Most families do not want to see their children working for long hours. Most would prefer to see them go to school, even if only for a few years. And certainly few would choose to send a small child away from home if alternatives were available. But many families desperately need the income children bring. Unless we solve the problem of family poverty, it will be difficult to end child labour.

When families live in desperate poverty, like these migrant labourers in Mumbai (Bombay), the extra income that children can earn may be crucial to their family's survival.

# The children's view

What do children themselves think about having to work? The fact is that it is very difficult to know. Child workers are often hidden from view and they are often frightened to talk to outsiders. Some working children may not even know what a different life could offer.

For the youngest children who work in the worst conditions, far from their families, life is very bleak. Many do not understand why their parents sent them away. Most dream of returning home with money or getting a better job with a kinder employer. Many say that they want to play and go to school like other children.

On the other hand, some children say that they are proud to be working and earning. At first they may give their wages to their parents but later many insist on keeping some earnings for themselves. Some children, especially those from violent or unhappy homes, are glad to live independent lives. These children need to be tough and streetwise to survive.

The situation of older children is more complex. In most countries teenagers work part-time, out of school hours or at weekends or during school holidays. In poorer countries many children leave school after primary school or drop out early. They must work to earn money for themselves and their family to survive. Whatever the law says, governments quietly accept that many older children are working. Banning them from working is usually not effective. Ill-thought-out **campaigns** against child labour can sometimes make things worse.

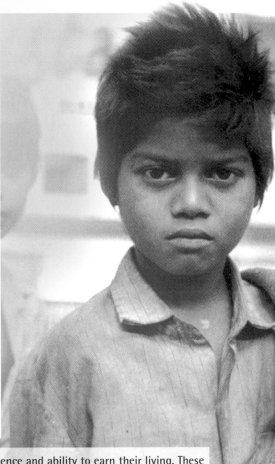

Some working children are proud of their independence and ability to earn their living. These boys live on the platforms of the largest railway station in Calcutta (now Kolkata), India.

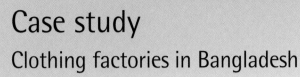

# Case study

## Clothing factories in Bangladesh

In 1992, the US **Congress** proposed to stop importing goods made by workers under fifteen years of age. The measure was aimed at clothing factories in Bangladesh, which mainly employed women and girls, some of whom were thirteen or fourteen. Although the girls begged to be allowed to keep their safe, regularly paid jobs, the factories began dismissing the youngest girls. Yet they still needed to work. Some became **domestic servants** or street workers – dangerous and unpleasant jobs. Rather than helping the children, the proposal made their situation worse. Later, it was agreed that the older girls could work full-time while the younger ones could work part-time while attending school. However, it is difficult to do well at school if you are already working.

# Does society benefit from child labour?

Who benefits from child labour? Some people certainly do. Uncaring employers who pay low wages to make extra profits and abusive parents who exploit their children for gain both benefit directly from child labour. But what about society as a whole?

## Child labour and economic growth

Some **economists** and historians point out that countries in Europe, North America and Asia used child labour in the early years of **industrialization**. They say that it is rational for **developing countries** to use cheap child labour, to compete with richer **economies**. Child labour helps to bring about the economic growth that will eventually result in higher living standards. As wages and conditions improve, parents will choose to send children to school rather than to work.

Other people argue that there is no proven link between child labour and economic growth. They say that a **developed economy** is built on education, skills, finance and changing technology, not cheap labour. Furthermore, most children do not work in growth industries such as computing, communications or science, but in agriculture, **domestic service** or on the streets.

# Child labour and society

But the economic argument is not the only one. Are there any other benefits, for society as a whole, from child labour? To become a healthy adult, a child needs good food, fresh air, space to play and opportunities to learn. These are not possible if children spend long hours at work in bad conditions. Instead their bodies become small and stunted, their eyes and ears are damaged by poor light or loud noise, their minds receive no stimulation. Many working children have little or no schooling and never learn to read and write. Some are killed or badly injured. Some are physically or sexually abused or are removed from their families – perhaps never to return. Many are forced to grow up fast, accepting adult responsibilities for younger children when they are still children themselves. Most people argue that under such circumstances, neither children nor society as a whole benefit from child labour.

Some children work in export industries, such as this carpet factory in India. But does society as a whole benefit from child labour?

# Laws against child labour

There are few governments today that openly support child labour. Many have banned it completely or restrict it to family farms or family businesses. Every country, except the USA and Somalia, has signed the **UN Convention** on the Rights of the Child, an agreement which lists children's human rights. (The USA says that it can support children without signing the Convention.) Over 130 countries, including the USA, have signed Convention 182 of the **ILO**, which calls for immediate action to get rid of the worst forms of child labour.

But while passing laws and signing international conventions is relatively easy, putting them into action can be very difficult. Governments need to appoint inspectors and re-train police officers and civil servants to act against offending employers. They must convince parents to send children to school rather than to work. Some governments simply do not have the skills or capacity to **enforce** the laws. Many governments lack the will to act and many are corrupt. Many governments act in favour of employers rather than children – the fact is that employers have money, influence and votes; children have none of these.

In India, with 100 million child workers, the government has signed over 120 ILO Conventions, all seeking to end child labour, including **bonded labour**. Yet child labour is widespread and openly acknowledged. Between 1986 and 1993, 4000 employers of children were brought before a court. Only a quarter were found guilty and not one went to jail. Many of the politicians who pass laws to protect children, and the judges and police who enforce them, have child servants at home and pass working children in the streets every day.

A few governments take no action against child labour, and some even use it themselves. In Myanmar hundreds of thousands of people have been forced to work for the army, without pay and in terrible conditions. Despite government denials, observers say that children are used as porters, messengers and labourers, and are worked the same brutal way as adults.

A boy in Bamako, Mali, displays a 'Red Card Against Child Labour'. The cards were distributed by the International Labour Organization at an African soccer tournament.

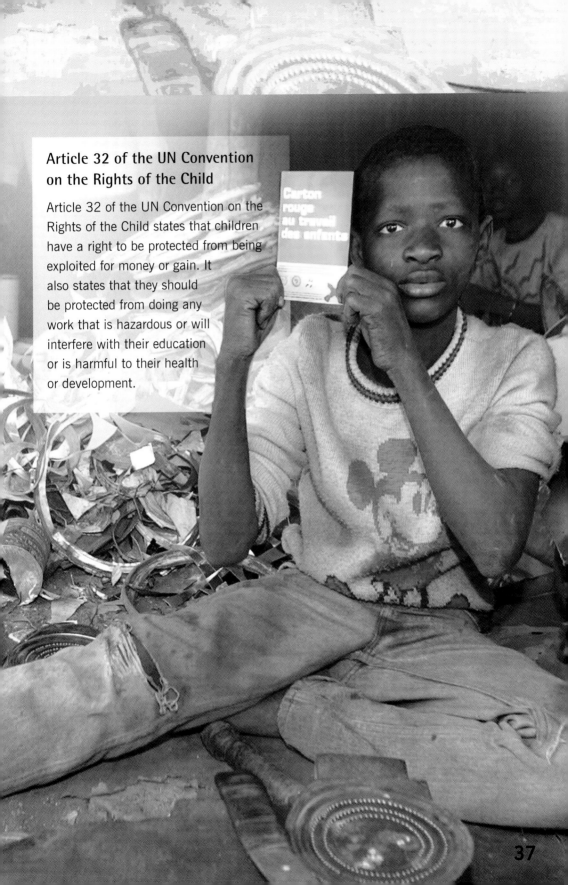

## Article 32 of the UN Convention on the Rights of the Child

Article 32 of the UN Convention on the Rights of the Child states that children have a right to be protected from being exploited for money or gain. It also states that they should be protected from doing any work that is hazardous or will interfere with their education or is harmful to their health or development.

# Organizing against child labour

In the 19th century opposition to child labour came from **campaigners** who wrote pamphlets, organized demonstrations and **lobbied** governments. Today, the driving force against **exploitation** of children comes from campaigners for children's and workers' rights. The difference is that today's struggles take place on a worldwide stage.

## Non-governmental organizations

In many countries, opposition to child labour comes from independent groups, known as **non-governmental organizations (NGOs)**. These range from small local groups to national organizations and international **coalitions**. Some carry out research and publish articles, some organize demonstrations and campaigns. Others give practical assistance to working children by providing meals, shelter, education and support. Some act to rescue children from **bonded labour** or **trafficking**, cruel employers or dangerous workplaces.

## Trade unions

**Trade unions** can also play an important role. While they rarely recruit children as members, they may support children in other ways. They call for increases in adult wages, so that families are less likely to send children to work to provide extra income. However, the impact of trade unions is limited because many governments ban or restrict trade unions, and many employers act ruthlessly to suppress union activity.

Working children join a demonstration against child labour in New Delhi, India's capital. They called on the government to take action to assist working children.

# Demonstrations and boycotts

NGOs, **consumer** groups and trade unions in wealthy countries have sometimes demonstrated against child labour in **developing countries**, especially where goods made by children seem to threaten local jobs or industries. Demonstrations and **boycotts** targeted against child labour can be effective. They may force importers to look more carefully at the farms and factories that supply their goods, and take steps to raise wages and improve conditions. However, this may lead to working children being thrown out of their jobs and on to the streets. NGOs, consumer groups and trade unions may help to improve the lives of some working children, but there are millions more they cannot reach. This is because they cannot solve the underlying problems of poverty that push children into work. That has to be the task of governments and the **UN**.

❝While millions of children are working, millions of adults are unemployed or do not earn enough to make a living. That is why we are convinced that one way to stop child labour is to ensure that their parents have access to decent jobs, decent wages and that their right to join and form unions is respected.❞

Bill Jordan, General Secretary of the International Confederation of Free Trade Unions (ICFTU)

# Education to end child labour

One of the key factors in ending child labour is providing more and better education. If children attend school, they cannot be in full-time work. Children who receive a good education will grow up to have more skills that can earn them more income. But this means that families and communities must value education and be prepared to keep children in school, rather than send them out to work.

These lessons come from history and from the present day. One of the most striking examples comes from India. In Kerala state, in southern India, education is taken very seriously. Every child attends school and almost everyone can read. Only one child in a hundred is working. In Bihar, in the north, education is not so highly valued and the schools are poorly equipped and badly run. Many children drop out of school early and never learn to read and write. In Bihar, one child in eight is working.

Why don't more children in places like Bihar go to school? There are many reasons. Older children stay at home to look after younger brothers and sisters while parents work. In some places there are no schools. Other schools hardly function, lacking books, desks or chalk and even the simplest equipment. Teachers go unpaid and classes are huge – classes of 60 or 80 children are common. And lessons are often irrelevant to pupils' lives. For many families the biggest single problem is poverty – they cannot afford to educate their children. Many governments charge fees for primary and secondary schools. On top of that there are costs

Even when classes are crowded, as in this school in India, children are keen to listen and learn.

for books, pens, uniforms and shoes. Making education affordable is vital.

In Uganda, the government was able to abolish primary school fees, enabling hundreds of thousands of poor children to go to school. But expansion has produced further problems. Uganda's schools are bursting at the seams and not all education is good quality.

# Primary education for all

Worldwide 130 million children aged 6 to 11 do not attend school; of these 80 million, roughly 60 per cent, are girls. Millions more children drop out of school early. Primary education for all children is one of the **UN Millennium Development Goals**, a set of targets to halve poverty by 2015.

In some countries there are special evening classes for children who must work during the day. This scene comes from Rajasthan, India.

# Ending poverty to end child labour

**❝We must move children to the centre of the world's agenda. We must rewrite strategies to reduce poverty so that investments in children are given priority.❞**

Nelson Mandela, former president of South Africa, 2002

Girls in Vietnam carrying water, a regular domestic task. When families have easy access to safe running water, children will be freed of such tasks.

Child labour is directly related to poverty. To end child labour, we need to end poverty. This is a massive task and poses the greatest challenge of our times. Poor countries need jobs and businesses, trade and **aid**. Poor children need families with secure homes, regular incomes and flourishing communities with schools and services (such as water and electricity). They need a real childhood of play, school and home – not long hours of work.

Sometimes simple changes can make a huge difference. Over a billion people lack clean, running water at an affordable price. Almost everywhere, water collection is the responsibility of women and girls. If they have to walk for miles, or wait for hours, to collect water, then women cannot do more productive work and girls cannot attend school. And if they must pay a high price for water, they are pushed further into poverty. So providing access to a

# Ending extreme poverty and hunger

About 1.2 billion people – one in five of the world's population – live in extreme poverty on less than US$1 a day; 2.4 billion live on less than US$2 a day. Ending extreme poverty and hunger is one of the **UN Millennium Development Goals**, a set of targets to halve poverty by 2015.

**Child labour and poverty exist hand in hand. Providing good housing, clean water and a healthy environment will give children a better life.**

safe, cheap water supply can help to reduce poverty and free children from hours of hard labour.

Despite the obstacles, some governments have made real strides in removing children from the fields and factories. For example, in Vietnam, the government has helped the poorest families to improve their standard of living and send their children to school. As a result, in the five years from 1993 to 1998, the numbers of working children fell by 28 per cent.

However, for every country that makes progress, others slip back. Wars and conflicts destroy families and communities, pushing children into work or even forcing them into armies. Millions of children have been orphaned by **HIV/AIDS** and have had to manage as best they can. Global action to end poverty is needed to make a difference.

# Child labour and you

What are the links between your life and the lives of the working children described in this book? They seem to be two different worlds. But look closer and explore ways that you can make a difference to their lives.

## Do some digging

Learn about the countries where child labour is a problem and speak to people in your own community to find out if child **exploitation** is a problem close to home. Find out about the companies which are likely to employ children. Be prepared to ask for more information if you think that a product is made by children. Write to the company, asking about wages, conditions and the minimum age of employment. Also ask if their factories are inspected, who does this and how often. Be persistent – many companies will not want to answer your questions.

A blind eleven-year-old Indian girl stitches a football. The balls sell for high prices in Europe.

## Look at the label

Some industries where child labour is widely used now label products made without child labour. For example, carpets produced without using child workers now carry a special 'rugmark' label.

## Pay a fair price

'Fair trade' products, such as coffee and chocolate, pay producers a good price and come from farms that do not use child labour.

## Write to your representative

Contact the person who represents you in government – your Member of Parliament or representative in **Congress**. Explain why you are concerned about working children and ask what your government is doing to end child labour worldwide. For example, are they helping poor countries to improve education or take children out of hazardous work? Are they taking action against **traffickers** of children or companies that exploit children.

## Give practical support.

There are many good **campaigns** to improve the lives of working children and groups that need your support. You could volunteer your time and collect funds for projects such as building day shelters, schools and training centres for working children – often a small amount of money can do great things. You can support working children directly through groups like the Global March Against Child Labour or Kids Can Free the Children.

## Remember the day

The **ILO** has declared 12 June each year as World Day Against Child Labour. What action can you take?

Happy, healthy children on the playing field. But did other children stitch the ball and sew their kit?

# Children paying the price

Look on the shelves of your local shop. Some of the items you see will have been produced by child labour. The **ILO** says that child workers are involved in growing crops such as cocoa, tea, coffee, cotton and rubber.

Take chocolate as an example. Chocolate is made from cocoa and 70 per cent of the world's cocoa is grown in Ivory Coast, Ghana and Nigeria in West Africa. The work is hard, conditions are poor and wages are low. Most of the workers are young men and boys, including 284,000 children. Some workers just get basic food and lodging.

The harvested cocoa is bought by big companies and shipped to Western countries (Europe and the USA) where it is turned into chocolate for sale. Yet only a tiny part of the price paid by **consumers** goes towards to the growers and workers. Much more goes into production, packaging and distribution and into profits for the retailer. The price paid to growers for cocoa has fallen sharply in recent years so workers' wages have fallen even further.

This unfair situation was highlighted by **campaigners** who pointed out that if companies paid higher prices for cocoa, and consumers paid higher prices for chocolate, then workers could receive higher wages. Living standards would rise and parents could afford to send children to school, rather than to work. In May 2002 chocolate manufacturers, human rights groups and the Ivory Coast government signed an agreement to try to end child labour on cocoa farms by 2005. Some chocolate manufacturers now pledge to pay a higher price for 'fair trade' cocoa that comes from farms that do not employ children.

Picking tea in Rwanda, East Africa. If consumers paid higher prices for tea, wages would be higher and children would not need to work.

# Case study

## Habib – hard work, heavy loads

Thirteen-year-old Habib works on a cocoa plantation in Ivory Coast. The work is hard – young boys wield sharp long knives and carry heavy loads. Habib arrived here with a group of boys from his village in Mali. It has become a well-worn trail – Mali is much poorer than Ivory Coast and many Malians seek work there. Yet Habib has never drunk a cup of cocoa or eaten a bar of chocolate. They are produced in factories overseas. Even if they were available, Habib would never be able to afford them.

# Ending child labour

Strong laws, active **campaigning** organizations, good schools, secure family incomes, growing **economies** – all have played a part in freeing children from the burdens and dangers of working. Today, it is widely accepted that no young child should have to work outside the family home and no child should ever have to do dangerous work.

Will we ever really end child labour? With almost 250 million children working worldwide, it is an enormous task. Millions of children must work to earn income and have no opportunity to attend school. Yet there are reasons for hope. Today, most of the world's children regularly attend primary school and many go on to secondary and college. These children do not need to spend their childhood in tiring labour.

The key to stopping child labour is to end extreme poverty in the communities where children have to work. Poverty is much more than just lack of money. It means lack of choices as well. It means people are forced to live hand to mouth, rather than thinking about longer-term goals, such as education, training and careers. So what is the world doing?

'Work is only for adults' – children in Ghana join the international movement to end child labour.

In September 2000, at the start of the new millennium, the **UN** adopted eight **UN Millennium Development Goals**, a set of targets to halve poverty by 2015. If the goals are achieved they will make a huge difference to working children.

The goals are:

1 End extreme poverty and hunger

2 Ensure a primary education for every child

3 Give equal treatment for girls and boys

4 Reduce deaths of babies and young children

5 Improve the health of mothers

6 Combat **HIV/AIDS**, malaria and other diseases

7 Protect the environment

8 Work in partnership for development

A few months later, in April 2001, UNICEF, the UN's children's organization, launched the Global Movement for Children. It called on all countries to adopt ten simple pledges to support the rights of all children.

1 Leave no child out

2 Put children first

3 Care for every child

4 Fight HIV/AIDS

5 Stop harming and **exploiting** children

6 Listen to children

7 Educate every child

8 Protect children from war

9 Protect the Earth for children

10 Fight poverty: invest in children

Eight goals, ten pledges, dozens of international conventions, thousands of laws worldwide – can they really make a difference to working children? Are they calls to action for a better future or empty promises? What do you think?

# Facts and figures

## Children aged 5–14 in work

| Region | Numbers | Percentage |
|---|---|---|
| Asia and the Pacific | 127,300,000 | 60.5% |
| Sub-Saharan Africa | 48,000,000 | 23.0% |
| Middle East and North Africa | 13,400,000 | 6.5% |
| Latin America and the Caribbean | 17,400,000 | 8.0% |
| Eastern Europe and the former USSR | 2,400,000 | 1.0% |
| Richest countries (North America, Western Europe, Japan, Australia) | 2,500,000 | 1.0% |
| **Total** | 211,000,000 | 100% |
| **Total children aged 5–17 in work** | 246,000,000 | |

## Children in work classed as hazardous

5–14 years of age: 111,000,000

15–17 years of age: 59,000,000

**Total 5–17 years of age:**

170,000,000

## Children in slavery

(**bonded labour**, **trafficking**, child soldiers etc.)

5–17 years of age: 8,400,000

Source: A Future Without Child Labour, International Labour Organization, 2002

## Work done by child workers

| Type of work | Percentage |
|---|---|
| Agriculture, fishing, forestry | 70.4% |
| Manufacturing | 8.3% |
| Shops and catering | 8.3% |
| Domestic and other service | 6.5% |
| Transport and communications | 3.8% |
| Construction | 1.9% |
| Mining and quarrying | 0.8% |

Source: A Future Without Child Labour, International Labour Organization, 2002

# Going to school

| Region | Children attending primary school | | Children attending secondary school | |
|---|---|---|---|---|
| | Girls | Boys | Girls | Boys |
| South Asia | 68% | 74% | 33% | 52% |
| East Asia and the Pacific | 95% | 95% | 60% | 66% |
| Sub-Saharan Africa | 54% | 58% | 22% | 28% |
| Middle East and North Africa | 76% | 84% | 55% | 64% |
| Latin America and the Caribbean | 92% | 92% | 53% | 49% |
| Eastern Europe and the former USSR | 80% | 82% | 82% | 82% |

Source: UNICEF, The State of the World's Children 2002

# International conventions related to child labour

**1926** – League of Nations Slavery Convention

**1930** – League of Nations Forced Labour Convention

**1948** – UN Universal Declaration of Human Rights

**1973** – ILO Convention 138 – Minimum Age Convention

**1990** – UN Convention on the Rights of the Child

**1999** – ILO Convention 182 – Elimination of the Worst Forms of Child Labour

# 'AIDS orphans'

The rapid growth of **HIV/AIDS** in Africa has created millions of 'AIDS orphans'. As parents and adult relatives die, grandparents and children have to take on the burden of supporting the family. 'AIDS orphans' find themselves digging and hoeing the ground, walking miles each day for water and looking after younger children – tiring tasks for an adult, let alone a child – while trying to come to terms with the loss of their parents. Most of these children say that they feel helpless and fear for the future.

# Further information

## Contacts in the UK and Ireland

**Anti-Slavery International (ASI)**
Thomas Clarkson House
The Stableyard, Broomgrove Road
London SW9 9TL
Tel: 020 7501 8920
email: info@antislavery.org
**www.antislavery.org**

**Save the Children Fund**
Mary Datchelor House
17 Grove Lane
London SE5 8RD
Tel: 020 7703 5400
email: enquiries@scfuk.org.uk
**www.savethechildren.org.uk**

**UNICEF UK**
64–78 Kingsway
London
WC2B 6NB
Tel: 020 7405 5592
email: helpdesk@unicef.org.uk
**www.unicef.org.uk**
**www.therightssite.org.uk**

**UNICEF Ireland**
25–26 Great Strand Street
Dublin 1, Republic of Ireland
Tel: (01) 878-3000
email: info@unicef.ie
**www.unicef.ie**

## Contacts in the USA and Canada

**Child Labor Coalition**
c/o National Consumers League
1701 K Street, NW, Suite 1200
Washington DC 20006
email: nclncl@aol.com
**www.nclnet.org/clc.htm**

**Fields of Hope (child agricultural labourers worldwide)**
email: info@fieldsofhope.org
**www.fieldsofhope.org**

**International Labour Organization (Washington office)**
1828 L Street NW # 600
Washington, DC 20036
email: washilo@ilowbo.org
**http://us.ilo.org/ilokidsnew/**

**Rugmark Foundation**
733 15th Street, NW, Suite 912
Washington, DC 20005
email: info@RUGMARK.org
**www.rugmark.org**

**US Fund for UNICEF**
333 East 38th Street
New York, NY 10016
email: webmaster@unicefusa.org
**www.unicefusa.org/**

**UNICEF Canada**
Canada Square
2200 Yonge Street, Suite 1100
Toronto, ON M4S 2C6
email: secretary@unicef.ca
**www.unicef.ca**

**Kids Can Free The Children**
Suite 300, 7368 Yonge Street
Thornhill, Ontario, L4J 8H9
email: info@freethechildren.com
**www.freethechildren.org**

# Contacts in Australia and New Zealand

**UNICEF Australia**
P O Box A2005
Sydney South
NSW 1235
email: unicef@unicef.org.au
**www.unicef.org.au**

**New Zealand Committee for UNICEF**
PO Box 10-978,
Wellington,
New Zealand
email: 2helpkids@unicef.org.nz
**www.unicef.org.nz**

# The Internet

**LearningChannel.org**
**www.learningchannel.org**

**Global March Against Child Labour**
**http://globalmarch.org/**

**NGO Committee on UNICEF**
**www.ngosatunicef.org**

**OneWorld (linking 950 organizations)**
**www.oneworld.net/**

**United Nations Children's Fund (UNICEF)**
**www.unicef.org**

# Further reading

*The Changing Face of Slavery* (Anti-Slavery International, 1997) Video and Teacher's Resource Book.

*Hidden Lives: Voices of Children in Latin America and the Caribbean,* Duncan Green (Latin America Bureau, 1998)

*India: Children's Needs: Children's Rights* (UNICEF UK, 1998)

*Liberating Children: Combating Hidden and Harmful Child Labour* (Department for International Development, 2002)

*'Child Labour', New Internationalist* (issue 292, July 1997)

*Poverty,* Kaye Stearman (Belitha Press, 2002)

*Slavery Today,* Kaye Stearman (Hodder Wayland, 1999)

# Glossary

**aid**
funds given by richer countries to poorer countries

**apprentice**
young person training to do a job

**benefits**
payments made by governments to people who are unemployed, ill or disabled

**bonded labourers**
people working for others to pay off a debt, often for years and in harsh, exploitative conditions

**boycott**
refusal to buy or handle goods, as a punishment or protest

**campaign**
work towards a goal in an organized way

**chimney sweep**
person who cleans chimneys

**coalition**
group of countries or organizations that join together for a common cause

**Congress**
law-making body, especially that of the USA

**consumer**
person who buys or uses goods or services

**convention**
legal agreement between nations

**developed economy**
wealthy, economically advanced country

**developing countries**
poor agricultural countries trying to raise living standards

**domestic service**
work performed by servants in a household

**economist**
expert in economics

**economy**
goods, services and technology produced by a society

**enforce**
make sure that something, such as a law, is complied with

**evangelical**
form of Christianity inspired directly by the gospels (the Bible) and especially concerned with converting non-Christians

**eviction**
order by authorities or a private landlord to leave an area or building

**exploitation**
making people work very hard and paying them little or nothing in order to make large profits

**handloom**
weaving machine worked by hand

**HIV/AIDS**
Human Immuno-deficiency Virus infection, leading to AIDS (Acquired Immune Deficiency Syndrome), an illness that destroys the body's protective systems

**hybrid**
offspring of two different varieties

**industrialization**
process of changing from an economy based on agriculture to one based on manufacturing

## Industrial Revolution

shift from an agricultural to a machine-driven manufacturing economy, usually referring to Britain (1780–1830 CE)

## International Labour Organization (ILO)

UN organization concerned with the conditions and rights of workers

## lobby

try to influence especially into taking politically significant action

## manufacturing

making goods on a large scale using machinery

## medieval

of the Middle Ages in Europe (approximately 1000–1500 CE)

## migrant worker

person who travels to work in another area or country

## minimum wage

lowest level of wages, set by government

## non-governmental organization (NGO)

not-for-profit organization that aims to help people

## pesticide

chemical used to kill insects that feed on crops. Pesticides are sometimes hazardous to people and the environment.

## plantation

large farm, usually growing one crop for sale and worked by labourers

## pollinating

fertilizing a plant with pollen

## radical

person with strong political views to do with social reform

## reformer

person who wants to make improvements and remove faults in society

## standardized

carried out so that products meet a certain standard and size

## strike

refuse to work, in order to win increased pay or better conditions

## trade union

group of workers joining together to improve wages or conditions

## trafficking

removing people by force or deceit from their community, imprisoning them and (sometimes) selling them, often in another country

## United Nations (UN)

international organization linking, and working for, all countries of the world

## UN Millennium Development Goals

targets to halve world poverty worldwide by 2015 (including having all children attend primary school)

# Index